BOSTON BOARD OF TRADE.

REPORT

OF A

SPECIAL COMMITTEE

UPON

MR. SENATOR SUMNER'S BILL,

PROVIDING FOR THE ISSUE OF

COMPOUND-INTEREST NOTES,

PRESENTED JANUARY 10TH, 1872.

BOSTON:
1872.
BARKER, COTTER & CO., PRINTERS,
14 STATE STREET.

BOSTON BOARD OF TRADE.

REPORT

ON

MR. SENATOR SUMNER'S BILL.

The Committee appointed to consider Mr. Sumner's bill for the substitution of compound interest notes in place of the present issue of legal tender notes, present the following report:

Before proceeding to the consideration of the subject specially assigned to the Committee, it may be useful to ascertain whether there is or is not an excess of paper circulation, a question upon which there exists much difference of opinion.

On the 1st of January, 1862, the date of the suspension of specie payments, the currency of the United States was substantially as follows:—

Bank circulation,		$183,792,079
Bank deposits,		296,322,408
Specie in bank,		102,146,215
Specie in Treasury, say,		6,000,000
Specie in hands of the public, say,		100,000,000
Treasury notes in circulation,		33,460,000
		$721,720,702
Deduct:		
Specie in bank,	$102,146,215	
Bank notes on hand,	25,253,589	
Cash items of banks,	27,827,971	
		155,227,775
Active circulation of the United States, January 1, 1862,		$566,492,927

Bank deposits being, by means of checks, the most actively circulating form of bank currency, should, of course, be included. Soon after this date, under the pressure of a supposed necessity, the legal-tender act of February 25, 1862 was enacted, and the emission of United States notes rapidly increased. The banks, being in a state of suspension, had every inducement to increase their issues of notes and thereby enlarge their profits by extended loans. The effect was soon apparent in rapidly advancing prices (in paper,) of all commodities, and the stimulus thus given to all speculative transactions. This state of things continued, with increasing issues by the Treasury, culminating in the summer of 1864, when the value of the United States greenback dollar had fallen to thirty-five cents in gold.

Our people seemed to be seized by a delirium of prosperity, and every one found himself to be growing suddenly rich without labor, except those unfortunates having fixed incomes or debts due them. These found that a formerly adequate income was diminished one-half in power to provide the means of subsistence, and that debts contracted in gold values were paid in a currency worth less than half of the promise. Fortunately, even for these there was one resource, and it was the means of preventing a vast amount of injustice and suffering. The currency which the Government compelled every creditor to receive at par, though really worth less than fifty per cent. for the purchase of most other kinds of property, was received by the United States at par, in exchange for its bonds, principal and interest payable in gold, and which the loyal people of the North fully believed would be so paid. Consequently, a vast amount of money received by mortgagees, trustees, savings banks, insurance companies and others, was thus invested, and the capital and income saved intact for the owners. But for this, ruin would have overtaken multitudes who have never known their danger.

When it is considered that the census valuation of the loyal States in 1860 was about ten thousand millions, and that an average advance of only fifty per cent. made an apparent gain of five thousand millions of dollars, it is not surprising that such a sudden accession of supposed wealth should have proved a source of intoxication, fruitful of the wildest extravagances. The sobor paths of honest industry present few attractions at such a time, and the ventures of the gold room and the stock exchange prove more alluring than the workshop and the counting room.

It is unnecessary for your Committee to enlarge upon the demoralization of such an experience. Every one can remember the thousand and one petroleum, mining and other companies that were "placed" during those years, and how ready the most conservative citizens were to swallow the gilded hook. The usual outgrowth of defalcations, forgeries and breaches of trust followed, and are still too frequent. Some of the victims are occasionally caught and imprisoned, while the real culprit, *a false measure of value*, is still at large, and finds too many to do him homage.

At the close of the war an important change had taken place in the currency of the United States, which stood about as follows:

[It should be remarked that this circulation was mainly confined to the loyal States.]

		October, 1865.
National bank circulation, ...		$171,321,903
State bank circulation, ...		78,867,575
National bank deposits, ...		549,081,254
State bank deposits, not large and not easily obtainable,		
Specie omitted, as substantially out of circulation.		
Legal-tender notes in circulation, (as given in report of the Controller of the Currency,) .		704,584,658
		$1,503,855,390
Deduct:		
Bank notes on hand, . .	$16,247,241	
Bank cash items, (checks not presented, etc.,) . . .	72,309,854	
Legal-tenders in bank, . .	193,094,364	
		281,651,459
Active circulation, October 1, 1865, . .		$1,222,203,931

In less than four years the currency had doubled. At this time the feeling of the country and of Congress was decidedly in favor of an early withdrawal of legal tender, and speedy resumption, as is shown by the resolution "pledging the House to coöperate with the Secretary of the Treasury in a contraction of the currency, with a view to the early resumption of specie payments," proposed in the House of Representatives by Mr. ALLEY, December 18, 1865, and which passed the House—144 yeas, 6 nays.

Merchants were holding light stocks, the spring importation had been small, and consumption was treading closely upon production. The southern market had been suddenly opened for large supplies of goods in exchange for cotton, which Europe was ready to buy at high prices. Unfortunately, more than one thousand millions of the public debt was payable, at the option of the holder, within three years, and the Secretary did not dare to attempt contraction until this large amount should have been funded. Thus was lost the golden opportunity, which will never return. Nevertheless, in 1866 and 1867, the maturing of the compound interest notes effected a contraction of two hundred millions, and the requirements of the Southern States caused a withdrawal of a large amount from the circulation of the North. Since 1867 no efforts in that direction have been made, and to-day the United States will offer nothing better for its promise to pay a certain sum of money to the bearer than another promise of the same tenor, possibly on cleaner paper. And yet we boast constantly that we are paying off the public debt which is not due for many years.

With many persons it is a favorite theory that if the volume of the paper issues be allowed to remain, the country will soon "grow up to specie payments." How long a process this would probably be may be inferred from a comparison of the average paper circulation *per capita*, for a series of years. In the finance report for 1865 appeared a statement made up by Dr. WILLIAM ELDER, of the Treasury department, as follows:

From 1825 to 1832, 8 years	. . .	$4.74 *per capita.*
" 1833 to 1836, 4 "	. . .	7.10 "
" 1837 to 1838, 2 "	. . .	8.35 "
" 1839 to 1845, 7 "	. . .	5.16 "
" 1846 to 1847, 2 "	. . .	5.08 "
" 1848 to 1853, 6 "	. . .	5.34 "
" 1854 to 1857, 4 "	. . .	7.30 "
" 1858 to 1860, 3 "	. . .	6.08 "

In this table the averages are given for the whole population, free and slave; the latter should properly be omitted, which would increase the averages rather less than two dollars *per capita.*

Compare the averages of legal tender and bank circulation since the war:—

In 1865	. . . . . .	$28.91 *per capita.*
1866	. . . . . .	24.38 "
1867	. . . . . .	21.00 "
1868	. . . . . .	18.86 "
1869	. . . . . .	18.32 "
1870	. . . . . .	17.40 "
1871	. . . . . .	17.80 "

It will be noticed that when the country was preparing for the panic of 1837 the average was but eight dollars and thirty-five cents, and for the four years prior to 1857 it was but seven dollars and thirty cents. If the issues of the last ten years had been of unsecured bank notes, there can be no doubt that the collapse would long since have taken place, but, being secured by the guarantee of the government, there can be no question of ultimate payment, and no food for panic on the part of the bill holders.

In this connection, the attention of the Board is called to the annexed abstract from the returns of the national banks, indicating a rapid expansion of bank credit. During the past year, it will be noticed that the deposits have increased by the enormous sum of one hundred and nine millions, and the bank loans during the same time one hundred and six millions, the latter showing a constant increase since 1866. Surely the pressure of a gentle contraction of government paper would exercise a most wholesome influence upon the banks, causing a gradual curtailment of bank credits.

In the judgment of your Committee, no good reason can be given to show that the country has use for double the amount of currency circulating in 1862. The population has increased about one-third, and it is not easy to see why the currency should increase in greater ratio. If it be said that the business and wealth of the country have largely increased, the reply is that the country never had a more prosperous decade than from 1850 to 1860, while the amount of bank circulation diminished from 6.69 a head in 1850 to 6.52 in 1860. In England, the bank act of 1844 provided against any increase of the paper circulation, excepting against an equal amount of specie in bank. Since that time the wealth and trade of Great Britain have enormously increased, yet there is no lack of currency. As they do not fill the currents with paper, their wants are supplied by the influx of gold. It will be remembered that while the average for thirty years prior to 1860 was about six dollars a head, the bank issues were unrestricted in many States, and the banks had every inducement to increase their profits by crowding to the utmost their bill circulation, and they were not slow to make the most of their opportunity.

The extension of the railroad system and of telegraphs, so far from creating demand for more currency, has the contrary effect, by economizing very much the use of it by giving greater rapidity of circulation, while the adoption of the national banking system has induced the general use of bank checks instead of bank bills, as a means of remittance.

It may not be amiss to allude briefly to the effect of an expanded currency upon our exports. When the expansion was going on in 1862, 1863 and 1864, our markets had greater or less supplies of exportable merchandise, produced at a cost resulting from a more restricted circulation. The fact that any thing that would realize abroad one dollar in gold could be made available here at the value of one dollar and fifty cents, two dollars or two dollars and sixty cents, in payment of debts, or investment in governments, caused the shipment of large quantities of produce, to be sold abroad at very low prices. Thus, during 1863, sound American flour of good brands brought, in Liverpool, but four dollars and thirty-six cents a barrel, after paying freight and charges, and American wheat sold at four shillings and nine pence, yielding less than one dollar a bushel, after paying charges.

The following table will show the effect of our large shipments in depressing prices at Liverpool:

	Wheat, per quarter. s. d.	Hams, per cwt. s. d.	Bacon, per cwt. s. d.
1860, ...	57.8	68.9	53.5
1861, ...	55.2	47.0	48.2
1862, ...	50.3	35.5	35.1
1863, ...	43.9	33.2	26.11
1864, ...	38.0	. . .	. . . .
Spring of 1865, ...	37.3	. . .	. . .

It will be seen at a glance, that although the shipper could save himself from loss by turning the exchange into currency and paying debts, the country suffered an enormous loss in sending abroad the products of labor, to be sold at hardly more than half the natural prices. But it was not in our shipment of produce alone that we were made to pay for our disregard of financial laws. The following quotations for a few American securities are taken from the London *Economist* of July 23, 1864: United States six per cent. gold bonds, forty-eight to forty-nine per cent.; Illinois Central seven per cent. bonds, first mortgage, fifty-five to fifty-eight; Michigan Central eight per cent. bonds, first mortgage, fifty-five to sixty; Michigan Southern seven per cent., first mortgage, forty-four to fifty-five; New York Central seven per cent., first mortgage, forty-four to fifty-five; Pennsylvania Central seven per cent., first mortgage, forty-four to fifty-five. When it is remembered that we have sent abroad, during the last ten years, our promises to pay at some future time amounting to more than one thousand millions of dollars, for which we have probably not received more than seven hundred and fifty millions, and of which the annual interest will nndoubtedly average not less than nine per cent. per annum upon the cost to the foreigner, we have one more item to add to the melancholy account of national waste.

When the inflation has had its effect in advancing the cost of production above the natural level, the country stands at still greater disadvantage, if possible, in its dealings with foreign nations. With all the products of our industry costing paper money prices, while the willingness of foreigners to take our bonds has depressed gold to within ten per cent. of par in paper, we come into the markets of the world utterly unable to compete with other nations, save only in raw materials, the results of the bounty of nature quite as much as of the industry of man. A nation of industrious, inventive, quick-witted workers, we owe the impotent part we are content to play in the commerce of the world mainly to the vain effort to delude ourselves with the idea that broken promises can ever be a standard of value or a safe medium for the discharge of honest debts.

It is sometimes claimed that a state of suspension is advantageous to the country, inasmuch as we are freed from the derangements which sometimes follow specie shipments in specie-paying times. But a demand for gold signifies merely that we are called upon to pay debts that we owe abroad. It is true also that a state of suspension for an individual would be a very convenient relief from the perplexities of a stringent money market, yet no solvent merchant would be willing to accept relief at such a price. It is to be hoped that no member of this Board will commend a course of action for his country which he could not accept for himself without personal dishonor.

Your Committee know of but one remedy for an over-issue of paper, and that is to withdraw it from circulation. This withdrawal may be involuntary, the result of a financial crisis, as in 1837 and 1857, or it may be gradual, as was the retirement of two hundred millions of dollars in 1865 and 1866 by means of compound interest notes. The advocates of the plan of drifting into specie payments frequently refer to the long suspension in England, from 1797 to 1821, as proof that nothing is wanting but time. But the ability of the Bank of England to resume was really due to the contraction caused by the failure of the country banks. According to McCulloch, there were about two hundred and eighty country banks in England at the time of the suspension in 1797. Then, as now, banking upon dishonored paper was profitable, and the number of banks had increased to above nine hundred in 1813. A heavy fall in the price of grain in 1814 proved ruinous to many farmers, so that a panic ensued, which caused the failure in

1814, 1815 and 1816, of no fewer than two hundred and forty banks, and this reduction of bank paper brought gold nearly to par, as will be seen by the following table, showing the average premium upon gold for the years

1812, . .	$20\frac{3}{4}$ per cent.	1817, . .	$2\frac{3}{4}$ per cent.
1813, . .	23 "	1818, . .	$2\frac{3}{4}$ "
1814, . .	25 "	1819, . .	$4\frac{1}{2}$ "
1815, . .	$16\frac{3}{4}$ "	1820, . .	$2\frac{3}{4}$ "
1816, . .	$16\frac{3}{4}$ "	1821, . .	par.

As an encouragement to hope for an improved state of morals after resumption, it may be stated that the convictions for passing forged paper of the Bank of England were: In 1816, one hundred and four; 1817, one hundred and twenty-eight; 1818, two hundred and twenty-seven; 1819, one hundred and ninety-three; 1820, three hundred and fifty-two; the year of resumption, 1821, one hundred and thirty-four; 1822, sixteen; 1823, six; 1824, five.

It is the belief of your Committee that in the slow and steady withdrawal of greenbacks lies the only safe mode of escape from the present unsound condition of the currency of this country.

This is what Mr. SUMNER's bill proposes to do. No other form of contraction is likely to be so flexible and automatic in its action. When money is abundant they will disappear; when the market is stringent they will circulate. For this reason the contraction will usually take place in the summer months. It will be observed that the measure is permissive, not compulsory. If, as is alleged, the present amount of currency is "needed by the country," these notes will all remain in circulation. Each holder of a note will know, better than any one can tell him, how much he needs it, and he certainly will not exchange it for a bond unless he prefers the latter. If the individual citizens are satisfied, the "needs of the country" may be safely left to take care of themselves. As the currency receipts of the Treasury are mainly in bank notes, it is doubtful if so large a sum as ten millions monthly can be obtained, and, in the judgment of your Committee, five millions monthly will be a sufficiently rapid contraction. Your Committee would suggest, also, that the Government should retain the option to pay in coin or bonds at the maturity of the notes. The Treasury would be in a much more independent position, and for the further reason that payment in coin, without a previous withdrawal of a large part of the whole issue of greenbacks, would probably lead to the outflow of gold from the country. In the transition to specie payments the country should be strong in gold; and this can only be attained by keeping it under lock and key until the excess of paper has been disposed of. Contraction as the means to specie payments, and not as the effect, is the only rule of safety. Your Committee recommend the adoption of the following resolutions:

Resolved, That the Boston Board of Trade approves the principle of the plan proposed by Mr. SUMNER in the Senate of the United States for the gradual withdrawal of the greenback circulation, and the substitution therefor of compound interest notes, in monthly issues of five millions, bearing interest at not less than four per cent. per annum.

Resolved, That the notes should be made payable at maturity in coin or bonds, at the option of the Government, and not at the option of the holder.

Respectfully submitted,

WM. ENDICOTT, JR.,
J. S. ROPES,
H. P. KIDDER,
B. F. NOURSE,
SAMUEL H. WALLEY,
JOHN GARDNER,
} Committee.

BOSTON, January 10, 1872.

	Oct., 1866.	Oct., 1867.	Oct., 1868.	Oct., 1869.	Oct., 1870.	Oct., 1871.
National and State Bank circulation.........	$289,877,583	$297,980,094	$298,675,841	$296,048,342	$298,297,245	$317,440,173
National Bank deposits.....................	596,911,346	565,670,423	601,830,278	523,029,491	517,598,331	626,774,021
Compound Interest Notes..................	155,512,140	78,839,580	5,251,930	......	......	......
Greenbacks in circulation..................	384,240,707	359,216,208	375,588,693	382,556,937	363,452,679	377,573,393
	$1,426,541,776	$1,301,706,305	$1,281,346,742	$1,201,634,770	$1,179,348,255	$1,321,787,587
Deduct Bank Notes on hand................	17,437,699	12,174,313	12,065,642	10,776,023	17,001,846	14,197,653
Cash items in Banks.......................	103,676,647	134,591,731	143,241,395	108,809,817	89,438,110	115,224,122
Legal Tender in Bank......................	205,770,641	157,439,049	99,229,996	85,810,022	80,673,268	109,083,150
	$326,884,987	$304,205,093	$254,537,033	$205,395,862	$187,113,224	$238,504,925
Active circulation........................	$1,099,656,789	$997,501,212	$1,026,809,709	$996,238,908	$992,235,031	$1,083,282,662
Bank Capital not invested in U. S. Bonds.....	None.	1,110,365	5,969,741	42,311,101	52,169,004	47,938,746
Bank Loans, (exclusive of Governments)......	603,247,503	609,675,214	657,668,847	682,883,106	725,515,538	831,552,210

APPENDIX.

MR. SUMNER'S BILL

TO AUTHORIZE COMPOUND-INTEREST NOTES AS A SUBSTITUTE FOR LEGAL-TENDER NOTES.

Be it enacted by the Senate and House of Representatives of the United States of America in Congress assembled,

That the Secretary of the Treasury is hereby authorized and directed to prepare for circulation compound-interest notes equal in amount to the outstanding legal-tender notes and fractional currency of the United States, and in all respects similar to those heretofore issued under the act approved March third, eighteen hundred and sixty-three, entitled "An act to provide ways and means for the support of the Government."

SEC. 2. That these notes, of different denominations, to the amount of ten millions of dollars, shall be dated on the first day of each month, commencing with the first day of July next ensuing, when the amount named shall be ready for issue, and then afterward on the first day of each month until the requisite amount has been furnished.

SEC. 3. That the notes thus provided shall be paid out for all disbursements of the Treasury, except those due in coin, so long as they are sufficient for the purpose; and if the whole monthly instalment is not thus disposed of, it shall be the duty of the Secretary of the Treasury to exchange the surplus for the present legal-tender notes, so far as practicable, that the full sum of ten millions may be put into circulation each month.

SEC. 4. That it shall be the duty of the Secretary of the Treasury to cause the destruction each month of legal-tender notes to an extent equal to the notes issued under this act.

SEC. 5. That the notes issued under this act shall, at the option of the holder, be convertible, at the end of two years, in sums of one hundred dollars or its multiple, into bonds of the United States, not having less than ten nor more than forty years to run, and bearing interest at the rate of five per centum, and the Secretary of the Treasury is hereby authorized to issue such bonds.

SEC. 6. That whenever these notes, or the bonds into which they may be converted, can be sold at par in gold, the Secretary of the Treasury may sell them in such sums as may be called for, and apply the proceeds in gold to cancel legal-tender notes as they are paid into the Treasury.

SEC. 7. That the notes issued under this act shall constitute no part of the legal currency reserve required of the national banks.

WASHINGTON, December 4, 1871.

www.ingramcontent.com/pod-product-compliance
Lightning Source LLC
LaVergne TN
LVHW020642110826
845149LV00004B/1321
* 9 7 8 1 4 1 8 1 9 0 2 9 3 *